The Replenishment Anointing

Keys for Living in Supernatural Increase

PATRICIA KING

The Replenishment Anointing

ENDORSEMENTS

Patricia King is one of the most generous and prosperous leaders that I know in the body of Christ. She has a heart to see the Body come into alignment with heaven. You will find that this teaching on *The Replenishment Anointing*, when activated, will stretch your faith to believe for more than enough!

This teaching carries a mantle of faith and will open up the realm of breakthrough for you! I encourage everyone to get this book for friends and family and see God break out in their faith, family and finances. You will not be disappointed!

John Perks
Founder,
Breakthrough Ministries

Patricia King is a clear, concise prophetic voice. She consistently articulates fresh revelatory truth from the heart of God. In this book, Patricia skillfully unveils a comprehensive understanding of the biblical approach to the powerful principle, *The Replenishment Anointing*.

This profound yet practical revelation can release hearing hearts to choose to agree with God and personally activate *The Replenishment Anointing* into their own lives. The choice to be full, complete, and believing for increase will destroy whatever appears to be lacking in our lives. Patricia has given us a more excellent path to healing, deliverance, and prosperity. As I read this book, it was with the deliberate intention to learn and apply the truth that was being revealed and, once again, I have discovered the powerful reality of choosing to agree with the Word of God.

When we passionately desire the benefits, we will embrace the procedure.

Dr. Clarice Fluitt

Author, Motivational Speaker,

Transformational Life Coach

Do you want *more* of God? Well, the truth is He has already given us all of Him and all of His Kingdom through the finished work of the Cross. What you really want, what we all really want, is more understanding of how to access and enjoy all that He has made available to us.

Patricia King's new book, *The Replenishment Anointing*, is an open door of revelation inviting you into a place of plenty where you not only can receive all that the Lord has given you, but also step into a continual flow of God's never-ending fullness of blessing, goodness, power, provision and more.

Like Moses before the Red Sea in Exodus 14 when God spoke to him to help him step into all that he had already been empowered with and received, the biblical insights that Patricia shares in this book will speak to you so that you can cross over into greater manifestation of Kingdom abundance here in the earth.

Robert Hotchkin
Minister, Author,
Media Host, Prophetic Voice

TABLE OF CONTENTS

Replenishment:

To make full or complete again, as by supplying what is lacking, or used up.

Anointing:

Empowered by the Holy Spirit.

.

You know of Jesus of Nazareth, how God anointed Him with the Holy Spirit and with power, and how He went about doing good ... for God was with Him.

—Acts 10:38—

The secret things belong to the Lord our God, but the things revealed belong to us and to our sons forever.

—Deuteronomy 29:29—

Chapter One

A LIFE-TRANSFORMING REVELATION

If God were to come to you and say, "Child, I am going to teach you to live in a supernatural dimension where everything you give out will be miraculously replenished to your account, with increase and multiplication, all the days of your life," would you eagerly long for Him to reveal to you His deep secrets and keys concerning this matter?

I have been sharing this God-given revelation and impartation regularly all around the world and I am constantly seeing immediate and sustained results in the lives of those who activate it. The Word of God is truth (John 17:17b) and therefore I have absolute confidence that if you receive this revelation and activate it, you will be blessed beyond measure as you discover yourself living in a realm of sustained miracles!

This book contains a glorious revelation – a powerful mystery that will set you on a path of miracle replenishment and increase in everything that pertains to you. This is not a one-time miracle. This is a perpetual miracle realm that God is offering you, one that will replenish and increase your physical strength, your love, your time, your provision, your gifts, your anointing, and anything else that flows from you to God and others.

IMAGINE ...

◊ You give money from your bank account and it is immediately replenished and increased.

◊ You sacrifice your time to serve a friend in need, then discover that your time was replenished supernaturally so that you now have copious hours to spare in order to fulfill all your own desires.

◊ You spend your strength on serving the Lord and others, and right when you are feeling emptied out there is a fresh wave of strength immediately filling you, even beyond what you experienced prior. You feel replenished, revitalized, and ready for more!

This revelation of replenishment anointing unto increase has your name on it! Jesus secured this blessing for you in the covenant that He cut on the cross between GOD and MAN two thousand years ago. This is one of the blessings mentioned in Scripture that pertain to life and godliness. This is a great and magnificent promise that you have access to. This is one of the spiritual blessings in the heavenly places that is yours in Christ!

> [2]Grace and peace be multiplied to you in the knowledge of God and of Jesus our Lord; [3]seeing that **His divine power has granted to us everything pertaining to life and godliness,** through the true knowledge of Him who called us by His own glory and excellence. [4]For by these **He has granted to us His precious and magnificent promises,** so **that by them you may become partakers of the divine nature, having escaped the corruption that is in the world by lust**. —2 Peter 1:2-4

> Blessed be the God and Father of our Lord Jesus Christ, **who has blessed us with every spiritual blessing in the heavenly places in Christ**. —Ephesians 1:3

The Word of God is powerful and contains layers and layers of revelation within its many verses. God has hidden secrets within His Word so that we will search them out. He wants us to find them. When we discover a revelation, it is ours and becomes part of our spiritual DNA that gets passed down to our descendants!

> **The secret things belong to the Lord our God, but the things revealed belong to us** and to our sons forever, that we may observe all the words of this law.   –Deuteronomy 29:29

Shortly after Jesus shared the parable of the sower and the seed, His disciples came to Him privately because they didn't understand the parable, but they desired to. They asked Him to grant them revelation and understanding. His response was:

> "To you has been given the mystery of the kingdom of God, but those who are outside get everything in parables."   –Mark 4:11

Jesus is looking for true seekers. If you seek, you will find. Look at this amazing promise Jesus gave us:

"For everyone who asks receives, and he who seeks finds, and to him who knocks it will be opened."   –Matthew 7:8

THE STEWARDSHIP OF REVELATION

When God reveals a treasure from His Word, it is imperative that we steward it well. Many receive witness in their spirits that a promise is from God, but they do not nurture or steward it and therefore it does not benefit them. Often I have seen instances where a believer will receive a promise from God or a profound revelatory insight from the Word but they don't allow the Word to go from surface belief to true faith that is anchored in their soul. When true faith is activated, there is an internal reality that cannot be rocked. You know that you know that you know! The Word lives within you, becomes alive and operative, and bears fruit.

For the word of God is living and active and full of power [making it operative, energizing, and effective]. It is sharper than any two-edged sword, penetrating as far as the division of the soul and spirit [the completeness of a person], and of both joints and marrow [the deepest parts of our nature]...   –Hebrews 4:12 (AMP)

When Israel was in Egypt they had been given a word from God regarding their deliverance from bondage and their entrance into the Promised Land. They heard the promise and believed it on the surface, but when adverse circumstances rose up and warred against the promise, they doubted, and lost faith quickly – the Word had not taken root. As a result they failed to secure the revelation, so it did not benefit them. They spent forty years in the wilderness and failed to enter their land, although the promise remained.

> Therefore, let us fear if, while a promise remains of entering His rest, any one of you may seem to have come short of it. For indeed we have had good news preached to us, just as they also; but the word they heard did not profit them, because it was not united by faith in those who heard.   –Hebrews 4:1-2

When you receive this revelation, meditate on the word until it becomes alive within you. Believe it and activate it. Faith without works is dead. The revelation will grow and produce great results for you.

When I received the insights on the replenishment anointing, I meditated on it every day until it became part of me. I activated it regularly with intentionality,

16

and it produced fruit. At first the fruit came slowly, but after a number of months the fruit burst forth almost immediately after I activated it. Sometimes the results literally blew my mind – I will share some awesome testimonies with you later.

I am excited for you, believing with you and for you that this revelation will have the same impact on you as it has had on my life. It is my blessing to pour it into you. I have already prayed for you to receive powerful enlightenment, faith, and impartation.

The revelation of the replenishment anointing unto increase is hidden in the Word for you to discover. Let's discover it together ... get ready for a powerful, life-changing impartation.

... and they picked up twelve full baskets of the broken pieces, and also of the fish.

—Mark 6:43—

Chapter Two

LOAVES, FISH, *AND* CHICKEN

Almost every Christian knows the story about the miracle of the loaves and fish. I want to show you some things in this portion of Scripture that you might not have seen before, so let's unpack it.

> [34]When Jesus went ashore, He saw a large crowd, and He felt compassion for them because they were like sheep without a shepherd; and He began to teach them many things.

> [35]When it was already quite late, His disciples came to Him and said, "This place is desolate and it is already quite late; [36]send them away so that they may go into the surrounding countryside and villages and buy themselves something to eat."

> [37]But He answered them, "You give them something to eat!" And they said to Him, "Shall we

go and spend two hundred denarii on bread and give them something to eat?"

[38]And He said to them, "How many loaves do you have? Go look!" And when they found out, they said, "Five, and two fish."

[39]And He commanded them all to sit down by groups on the green grass. [40]They sat down in groups of hundreds and of fifties.

[41]And He took the five loaves and the two fish, and looking up toward heaven, He blessed the food and broke the loaves and He kept giving them to the disciples to set before them; and He divided up the two fish among them all.

[42]They all ate and were satisfied, [43]and they picked up twelve full baskets of the broken pieces, and also of the fish.

[44]There were five thousand men who ate the loaves.   –Mark 6:34-44

A large crowd of 5,000 men (some women and children were most likely present, though they aren't mentioned) had been listening to Jesus teach all day, and it was getting late. The disciples suggested to Jesus that they dismiss the meeting in order for the people to go into the nearby villages to get something to eat.

But Jesus' response was, "**You** give them something to eat."

Yikes! I can imagine the shock on their faces as they attempted to calculate what it would take to feed such a multitude – that would be a major catering event! Not only that but they were in a desolate place. Where were they going to get the food? Their response was interesting, and it is important to note. Immediately they responded with concerns about money. "Shall we go and spend two hundred denarii on bread?" The disciples did not need money for the people. They needed food. Jesus did not say anything about money. He said, "You give them **something to eat**." Their need was for food and not for money.

Money is a worldly currency. You will not find it in heaven. So often we equate our prosperity and wellbeing with how much money we have, and yet there is no promise in the Scripture that says God will give us money (although He is well able to do it and does not have a problem with providing it if needed). The Scripture promises that God will meet all our NEEDS according to His riches in glory in Christ Jesus (Philippians 4:19). Money is overrated and we are not to love it, worship it, or serve it. One day, the world's monetary system will come crashing down, but God's provision will never weaken or diminish. The miracle they needed at that moment had nothing to do with money – it was about food!

If you need food, ask for food. You don't necessarily need money to obtain food. God can give food directly. Jesus taught us to pray, "Give us this day our daily bread" (Matt. 6:11). If you need clothes, ask for clothes. We shouldn't equate everything we need to money.

A few years back, I had a car that I really enjoyed. It had low mileage, I had looked after it well, and I was very happy with it. One day, the Lord spoke to me and led me to give it to a friend who had been praying for a vehicle. He also said, "I am going to give you an upgrade." That all sounded amazing to me so I called my friend and drove her to the motor vehicle branch and transferred the car to her. She was touched by the goodness of God as He answered her prayer and blessed her. She did not need money, she needed a car, and that is what God provided.

As a result of that awesome transaction, I now had a need. I needed transportation but had no vehicle. The "upgrade" did not manifest right away, so I prayed every day for God to meet my need of transportation.

22

I didn't need money and, although the Lord had promised an upgraded vehicle, I did not actually need a car; I needed transportation. For 14 months I had supernatural provision of transportation every day. Whenever I needed to go somewhere, my chariot would arrive. One day, someone came to the door and said, "I was driving in your area and sensed the Lord say you needed a ride, so I came by to check." I did need a ride, and the Lord fulfilled that need. For over a year my transportation was divinely provided and I didn't need to cover monthly expenses for gas, insurance, or maintenance … and I had personal chauffeurs. It was glorious. I never lacked. Then, my upgrade finally manifested – a beautiful high-end vehicle that was perfect for my needs and completely paid for. The Lord was teaching me to believe Him specifically for what I needed.

If you have a mindset that money is what will meet your needs, you will get trapped in the land of "not enough". This is what happened to Israel when they were slaves in Egypt. The reason they were oppressed was that they had forgotten who they were. They were God's covenant people but living like slaves. Instead of looking to God for their provision they allowed the Egyptian world system to oppress them. They had been blessed by God in Egypt since the days of Joseph. They were multiplying quickly and Pharaoh was concerned, so he purposely implemented a plan of oppression to stop them from being prosperous and blessed. He made them work harder for less and enslaved them. They were enslaved under the money system.

This is what is happening in many western nations today. We have lived well and enjoyed the blessings of abundance, but we have become deceived by a monetary system. I hear many Christians say things like, "I'm in debt, I don't have enough money to make ends meet, I can't serve God because I am broke, I have a limited income…"

How did we get to this place? Unfortunately, we have trusted in a monetary system, but God wants us to turn back to Him. He clearly teaches us that we cannot serve God and mammon (the demonic monetary system). Money itself is not evil, but the love of it is. Money is not what gives us our security – God does.

The disciples were asking Jesus about money but His response was, **"How many loaves do you have? Go look."** In other words, "Let's not talk about money; they need food. They can't eat denarii, they need bread. How many loaves do you have?"

They went and looked. This is key. Oftentimes we think we don't have what it takes to meet our need but we overlook the provision that is already in our midst that God can use for a miracle. Look. You always have something to give – your catalyst for a miracle. The disciples went and looked and came back with five loaves and two fish. I'm sure they were wondering what Jesus was going to do with that little bit of provision in the presence of such a great need.

HERE COMES THE MIRACLE

Jesus was not discouraged by the seemingly insignificant offering that was brought to Him but, rather, He immediately prepared for a miracle. With great expectation, He organized the people into groups of 50s and 100s so they would be ready to receive the miracle food. One of the keys to working a miracle is to EXPECT a miracle.

Jesus then took the five loaves and two fish and looked towards heaven. This is another important key to note:

As a believer you are not an earthly being trying to get into heaven. You are a heavenly being living in the earth.

Be heavenly minded. Jesus knew that in the natural realm five loaves and two fish would not feed 5,000, but in God, all things are possible. He didn't look to the earthly realm for provision, He looked to the heavenly dimension – to the miracle realm. We need to turn our attention more to that dimension while living in the earth. Jesus taught us to pray, "Your kingdom come, Your will be done on earth as it is in heaven."

As He is looking to the heavenly realm, He BLESSES the food in His hand. Often we curse our provision. We say things like, "I don't have enough; I don't have what I need," or "How am I going to make ends meet?" Your words will bless or curse. Make sure you are committed to blessing your provision even if it doesn't look like it is enough to meet the need. Jesus didn't say, "Oh, Father, I am in a pickle here; there are over 5,000 people to feed and I have this measly little bit of bread and a couple of little fish – I'm in big trouble." No! He blessed the provision in His hand.

At this point, no miracle has yet taken place. The Scripture explains that after He blessed it, He broke the loaves. I am imaging that His twelve disciples distributed the bread and fish, so He had to break it up in pieces to give each of them some to distribute. **Now, here comes the big key for the miracle: He kept giving!**

He broke the bread and **kept giving** what was in His hand. I believe that He gave the pieces of bread to the disciples and they distributed it to the people.

The catering truck did not show up with a massive load of fresh bread and fish!!! Often people are waiting for some big lump sum of money to show up in order to meet their need, but with replenishment miracles it works differently. Some will say, "When my ship comes in, then I will give to the needs of the poor." That ship might never come in. If you are not giving what is in your hand, you might never see a miracle. Watch how the miracle took place:

Each disciple took his handful of bread to the first person and offered them something to eat. The person took the bread, emptying the disciple's hand, but by the time the disciple went to the next person the bread had been REPLENISHED. He gave out the bread to that person and it was REPLENISHED for the next one and then it was REPLENISHED for the next one and the next one and the next one. As long as they kept giving, the REPLENISHMENT anointing operated. The miracle was not the appearance of a big truckload of bread! The miracle was in their hand – everything they gave from their hand was REPLENISHED. Jesus didn't call forth the angels of heaven, and kaboom

– bread appeared! That could happen, of course, but that is a different type of miracle.

Jesus was teaching His disciples how to work the REPLENISHMENT anointing. But it gets better! Somewhere along the line, **it not only is replenished, but the provision increases**. They had to find baskets to put the overflow in. They started with a handful of bread, but as they kept giving, it INCREASED. At the end of the feeding program, 5,000 men – and probably some women and children – had eaten, and there were twelve baskets left over. They all ate and were satisfied – and all this without the catering truck!

Replenishment works as you give. Whatever you give gets replenished unto increase as you keep giving.

CHICKEN, CHICKEN, CHICKEN

Years ago, when our children were young, we lived near a lake that would freeze over in the winter. I stayed home one Sunday after church to cook our Sunday chicken dinner while my husband took our sons to skate on the lake. My husband met some friends and family members while skating and invited them all back for dinner. These were the days before cell phones. He arrived with 15 guests … *19 people for dinner, including our family … and one chicken.* I was somewhat

28

panicked, so as my husband was setting up an expanded table to seat our guests, I was praying hard (like, almost travailing) over the chicken. Just that morning I had read the story of the multiplication of the loaves and fish in my devotion time. I cried out to God for a similar miracle to take place with the chicken. Then I sliced it up in small pieces, hoping that everyone would be careful so we could maybe make it stretch.

At the table, I asked the blessing on the food (did I ever bless it!) Then I passed the platter to the first person on my left, who took a large portion of chicken off the plate. I silently gasped within, wondering how it was going to stretch to feed the others. The next person also took a generous portion, as did the next one. I was beside myself ... they continued to pass the platter and everyone heaped generous servings of chicken on their plates. However, about half way around the table I noticed that there was seemingly the same amount of chicken on the platter as we had started with. It was REPLENISHING. The platter went all the way around the table and was still full of chicken. Some guests had second helpings and some had thirds but there was still a full platter of chicken at the end of the evening. In fact, that chicken lasted three days. Our family ate chicken sandwiches, chicken casseroles, chicken stew ... chicken, chicken, chicken. REPLENISHMENT and INCREASE!

A few years later while on the mission field, we often saw the same replenishment miracle when we were feeding the poor.

When God created mankind, He blessed us with the ability to be fruitful (increase) and to replenish.

> And God **blessed** them, and God said unto them, Be **fruitful**, and **multiply**, and **replenish** the earth.   –Genesis 1:28 KJV

This is available to you, and the Lord wants you to move in this anointing as a natural part of your life. You are blessed by God to be fruitful, to multiply (increase), and to replenish!

Jesus taught His disciples more than once about this anointing. We see Him instructing the disciples on the replenishment anointing in the feeding of the 5,000 in Mark 6, but then again in Mark 8 He instructs His disciples with the feeding of the 4,000. A few verses down from that account, we find Jesus giving them a warning about unrighteous leaven. They thought He was upset because they forgot to bring bread on the boat. He responded to them with this rebuke:

> [17]And Jesus, aware of this, said to them, "Why do you discuss the fact that you have no bread?

Do you not yet see or understand? Do you have a hardened heart?

[18]"HAVING EYES, DO YOU NOT SEE? AND HAVING EARS, DO YOU NOT HEAR? And do you not remember, [19]when I broke the five loaves for the five thousand, how many baskets full of broken pieces you picked up?" They said to Him, "Twelve."

[20]"When I broke the seven for the four thousand, how many large baskets full of broken pieces did you pick up?" And they said to Him, "Seven."

[21]And He was saying to them, "Do you not yet understand?"   –Mark 8:17-21

Sometimes we do not have a truth established in us by just listening to it once. The disciples not only heard the instruction concerning replenishment but they also worked the miracle with Jesus. The miracle flowed through their own hands, but they still didn't get it.

Jesus wants you to know how to work replenishment miracles. Absorb the teaching and then activate it. You will see replenishment miracles work for you your entire life, if you believe.

The bowl of flour was not exhausted nor did the jar of oil become empty, according to the word of the Lord which He spoke through Elijah.

—1 Kings 17:8-16—

Chapter Three

REPLENISHMENT MIRACLES FOR THE WIDOWS

We also see the miracle of replenishment working through Elijah as he ministered to the widow at Zarephath.

[8]Then the word of the Lord came to him, saying,

[9]"Arise, go to Zarephath, which belongs to Sidon, and stay there; behold, I have commanded a widow there to provide for you."

[10]So he arose and went to Zarephath, and when he came to the gate of the city, behold, a widow was there gathering sticks; and he called to her and said, "Please get me a little water in a jar, that I may drink."

[11]As she was going to get it, he called to her and said, "Please bring me a piece of bread in your hand."

¹²But she said, "As the Lord your God lives, I have no bread, only a handful of flour in the bowl and a little oil in the jar; and behold, I am gathering a few sticks that I may go in and prepare for me and my son, that we may eat it and die."

¹³Then Elijah said to her, "Do not fear; go, do as you have said, but make me a little bread cake from it first and bring it out to me, and afterward you may make one for yourself and for your son.

¹⁴"For thus says the Lord God of Israel, 'The bowl of flour shall not be exhausted, nor shall the jar of oil be empty, until the day that the Lord sends rain on the face of the earth.'"

¹⁵So she went and did according to the word of Elijah, and she and he and her household ate for many days.

¹⁶The bowl of flour was not exhausted nor did the jar of oil become empty, according to the word of the Lord which He spoke through Elijah.   −1 Kings 17:8-16

Elijah was told by the Lord that a widow in Zarephath would provide for him. He went in obedience to the Word of the Lord to Zarephath and found the widow – but, my goodness, she didn't have faith to even provide for herself and her son, let alone the prophet!

When Elijah asked her for a piece of bread, she responded by saying something like, "Sorry, I would love to help you but all I have is a handful of flour and a little oil, so I am going to make my son and myself a piece of bread from it and then we are going to die." She only had faith to eat her last bit of provision and then die.

Elijah knew she wasn't going to die, because the Lord had told him the widow would provide for him. He had faith for a miracle of replenishment and led her right into the miracle. He directed her to go ahead and prepare the bread but to bring it to him first. The reason he needed her to bring it to him first is because he had the replenishment anointing operating. If he blessed that bread it would replenish. He had faith for this. If she ate the bread made from the last bit of flour and oil, she and her son would die according to her expectation.

She did as the prophet instructed and gave the bread she prepared to the prophet. Then she went back to the kitchen – replenishment had taken place! If she used up the handful of flour and oil to make the bread for the prophet, there would have been none left for her and her son, outside of a miracle. But, the replenishment anointing had kicked in and every time she went to make bread, flour and oil were replenished. This continued throughout the entire drought and famine. The widow provided for herself, the prophet, and her household through daily replenishment miracles, until rain came. Again, notice that the miracle occurred as she kept giving. She didn't have a semi truck of flour and oil show up. The Scripture mentioned that "she and he and her household ate for many days." Her household might have included not only her son but other relatives and servants that might have been with her. Everyone in her house was looked after during the drought and famine. That's not only replenishment – that's increase!

I admire this widow, because she could have withheld her final meal and kept it for herself and her son, but instead she gave it to the prophet. Her giving was the launching of her miracle.

In the replenishment miracle of the loaves and the fish, in one of the accounts it says a lad gave his lunch. He could have withheld it and looked after himself, but he gave it. I wonder if the twelve baskets left over went to him?

"Give, and it will be given to you. They will pour into your lap a good measure – pressed down, shaken together, and running over. For by your standard of measure it will be measured to you in return."   –Luke 6:38

ELISHA HELPS A WIDOW

[1]Now a certain woman of the wives of the sons of the prophets cried out to Elisha, "Your servant my husband is dead, and you know that your servant feared the Lord; and the creditor has come to take my two children to be his slaves."

[2]Elisha said to her, "What shall I do for you? Tell me, what do you have in the house?" And she said, "Your maidservant has nothing in the house except a jar of oil."

[3]Then he said, "Go, borrow vessels at large for yourself from all your neighbors, even empty vessels; do not get a few.

[4]"And you shall go in and shut the door behind you and your sons, and pour out into all these vessels, and you shall set aside what is full."

[5]So she went from him and shut the door behind her and her sons; they were bringing the vessels to her and she poured.

⁶When the vessels were full, she said to her son, "Bring me another vessel." And he said to her, "There is not one vessel more." And the oil stopped.

⁷Then she came and told the man of God. And he said, "Go, sell the oil and pay your debt, and you and your sons can live on the rest."

–2 Kings 4:1-7

What a difficult situation this widow was in! She was in debt and about to lose her two children to the creditors. It doesn't get much more grim than that! The replenishment anointing, however, saved the day!

Elisha asked her what she had. When we are in need, it is easy to look at what we don't have rather than what we do have. In the account of Jesus feeding the 5,000, when He first asked the disciples to provide food, they came back with the wrong answer. They were baffled because they did not see available provision to meet the need. Jesus told them to "go look." They came back with five loaves and two fish. The widow at Zarephath didn't think she had anything either, but the miracle was launched through the little she had, not through what she didn't have. You might think you are lacking, but go look – there might be more available to you than you think. Your miracle might be right in front of you … in your hand.

The widow in Elisha's situation said that all she had was a jar of oil. That was it! Elisha was acquainted with the replenishment anointing. He started administering the situation so she was ready for her miracle. He instructed her to borrow as many vessels as she could find. When she couldn't find any more, she started pouring the only oil she had into the next vessel. When she did that, her jar of oil was replenished. She poured it into the next vessel and it was replenished again. Every time she poured into another vessel, the oil replenished until there were no more vessels to pour into. As soon as the giving stops, the replenishment stops.

Once all the jars were full, Elisha instructed her to go and sell the oil. Now we see the extravagant increase. Not only had the oil been replenished, but there was so much increase that she could fully pay off her debt – but she also was blessed with an abundant overflow to live off. She had way beyond what she needed.

REPLENISHMENT AND INCREASE!

KEYS TO RELEASING THE
REPLENISHMENT ANOINTING

As we review all three of the scriptural examples shared previously, we discover the following keys to unlocking the replenishment anointing that is in you.

1. **Go Look!** When in need, don't look at what you don't have, look for what you do have, even if it seems insignificant. Celebrate the small, for it might be the catalyst for your miracle.

2. **Cultivate Expectation** and prepare for your miracle. Jesus began to seat the crowd in groups of fifties and hundreds. The widow at Zarephath baked the prophet's bread from her last bit of flour and oil. The widow Elisha had ministered to went out and got vessels in order to prepare for her miracle.

3. **Be Heavenly Focused.** The natural earthly dimension does not contain your miracle. The miracle realm is God's heavenly dimension visiting the earth. Set your mind on the supernatural. Whatever you focus on, you will empower!

4. **Bless Your Provision.** Proclaim blessing over your provision. Do not curse it with negative words, murmuring, or complaining.

5. **Keep Giving.** When in need, never withhold. A withholding spirit will cut off your supply. Keep giving in faith, with expectation for replenishment and increase.

May the Lord, the God of your fathers,
increase you a thousand-fold more than
you are and bless you, just as
He has promised you!

—Deuteronomy 1:11—

Chapter Four

TESTIMONIES

When this revelation filled my heart, I meditated on it regularly and put it into practice. Every time I gave, I commanded replenishment. Don't just be a hearer of the Word – be a doer of the Word. Faith without works is dead!

REPLENISHED STRENGTH

A while back I felt drained of strength after a long day of work. I had woken up at around 5:00 a.m., had my devotion time, got ready, put the house in order, ran off to a meeting at 7:30, another one at 8:00, and then attended back-to-back intense planning meetings until late afternoon – then an individual in crisis needed ministry. As a result, I got home at around 6:00. I felt like I wanted to have a hot bath and go to bed, but we had an evening engagement booked and I needed to be ready for company before 7:00. I found myself groaning in self-pity over my lack of strength, but then I remembered the replenishment anointing. I declared, "I have given and given and given of my strength all day, so I now receive replenishment for the evening." Immediately, my strength returned and I was gloriously refreshed. We ended up being up until after 11:00 that night, and I was fresh as a daisy the entire evening. REPLENISHMENT ANOINTING.

REPLENISHED TIME

When you give your time to serve God and others, your time can be replenished and increased. A number of years ago, I had worked an entire day on administration. There was big heap of things to take care of on my desk. After an entire day, the pile was still as high as it was when I started. That was not the kind of replenishment I wanted! It seemed that every piece I picked up to work on created more work, so the mountain wasn't moving. I was somewhat discouraged. I looked at the clock and it was 5:00 p.m. My husband and I had plans for dinner at 6:00, and then I needed to pack for an early morning flight the next day. Besides, it was "crime show night" and I wanted to watch my favorite crime show. I looked at the pile of work on my desk and thought, "I'm going to be here all night!"

The Lord spoke to my heart in the midst of my moaning: "You have given your time to Me each day – hours every day. All that is 'seed' that has been deposited into your heavenly bank account and is available with interest. What you sow, you will reap. All you need to do is make a withdrawal by faith."

That revelation was so insightful. I could have my time replenished because I had given time. I received by faith the time I needed to complete all that I had to do. I did not feel or sense anything, I just went back to work on the mountain. laboring through one piece at a time. Before I knew it, the pile was finished. I looked at the clock and it was not quite 6:00 yet. I was able to have dinner with my husband, pack, and … watch the crime show (by the way, I think some crime shows are very beneficial in cultivating a sense of justice and to stir intercession – smile).

REPLENISHED CLOTHING

In 1980, my husband and I, along with our children, went to YWAM in Kona, Hawaii. I took quite a few clothes with me, but while there I noticed several longer term workers did not have new clothes, so I gave almost all of my wardrobe away. I kept three garments to come home with.

That winter I was invited to speak at three meetings, but I didn't have a nice dress to wear (back in those days, we ministered in dresses). I prayed and asked the Lord for a dress. He not only furnished me with one dress, but three of them! After the events, I gave them away also, and that was the beginning of seeing replenishment anointing. Some mornings I would get up and open our front door to pick up the paper and a box of clothes would be sitting on the porch with the most perfect outfits and sizes. People would give me clothes, jewelry, and other accessories, and every time I gave, it would all be replenished unto increase.

I remember that when we started our outreach center in Tijuana, Mexico, in 1985, many on our team gave all the clothes that we had packed to the poor. We kept the outfit we were wearing and a change of clothes. God kept replenishing our supply of clothes to give to the poor, but also our own wardrobes. It was amazing to watch God at work in that way!

Over the years, every time we bought a new house we would always need a bigger closet. I couldn't give clothes away fast enough. I try to give some clothes away every 3-4 months, and they keep replenishing and increasing.

One year at our Women on the Frontlines World Convention, I emptied my closet of almost all my clothes. I packed up 110 outfits plus jewelry, handbags, shoes, and accessories, and then set up a boutique one day to let our partners come in and shop without money. It was so much fun.

My husband looked at my almost empty closet and commented, "Well, this is surely a sign and wonder." We finished the event on Saturday night, and by Monday morning a business owner in town had called me over to visit their shop; they gave me ten outfits from wonderful boutiques – each one beautifully bagged. That was the beginning of my replenished wardrobe after the World Convention. In less than two months my closet was full again! REPLENISHMENT AND INCREASE.

REPLENISHED FINANCES

I see finances replenished on a regular basis. It is so much fun! At one event, I had sown a $555 offering, a cash offering of $42, and a special offering of $1,000.

Before I left the event, someone came up to me and gave me a check. They said, "This is for you personally; it is not for the offering." I thanked them for the gift and put it in my handbag. A little later, someone else came to me with a wad of cash and said the same thing. Later that day, two more people came and gave me personal checks. I thanked them all and put the gifts in my handbag.

Later that night when I was emptying my handbag, I opened the gifts. The first check was for $1,000. That replenished the $1,000 special offering I had given earlier that day. The wad of cash was $555 which replenished to the penny the offering I had given that morning. And the two personal checks were $100 each which replenished unto increase the $42 cash offering. Before the day was out, all had been REPLENISHED AND INCREASED.

But it gets even better. The Monday following the event, my husband went to the mailbox and brought back a card from some friends in a different nation. It was a beautiful thank you note of appreciation, and in it was a personal check for $10,000. Needless to say, I was blown away! God is so good, and this replenishment anointing is real.

Sometimes when we have extra expenses and give extra extravagant offerings, the bank accounts empty out. I just open my computer to online banking and speak replenishment over the bank balances and they come right back up in no time. It is amazing.

I have had situations numerous times where I have given an offering in a meeting or to an individual, and declared replenishment over it, and before the next meeting it is replenished.

When I preach this message, we always have testimonies of miracles ... so many of them. There have been major business deals go through, debts paid off and other areas of breakthrough. It is a normal occurrence to have people come up after this message and share how they gave an offering in the meeting and it was replenished and increased before the day was out. I believe YOU will have testimonies like these, too, as you activate this anointing.

Sometimes the replenishment and increase has come immediately, and other times I have had to wait for it, but it always comes. I stand on the Word and believe it, and it manifests. Oral Roberts used to proclaim a quote from Smith Wigglesworth: "God said it. I believe it. That settles it." That's my testimony, too, and I'm sticking to it. Jesus taught this replenishment anointing to His disciples, and He is teaching it to you and me afresh right now. He so wants you to have this realm of the miraculous operating in your lives. The more you can bless others, the more you are blessed.

You were created to be blessed and to be a blessing. My prayer is that you will look for ways to give to the Lord and to the needs of others each and every day, and that you will cultivate this amazing replenishment anointing. This beautiful anointing is in you because He is in you!

Go with this anointing and bless the world you live in.

Be greatly replenished in all that you pour out, and experience increase beyond measure!

I am in your cheering section and releasing impartation to you!!! Go for it and activate this amazing, outrageous anointing for His glory right now!

ACTIVATION RESOURCES:

Decrees

Record of Replenishment Miracles

Suggested Courses & Books

I DECREE IN JESUS' NAME THAT:

1. I was created to be fruitful and multiply. (based on Genesis 1:28)

2. I do not fear and I am not anxious concerning material needs, for I am confident that my God will care for me as I seek first His kingdom and His righteousness. (based on Matthew 6:33)

3. All my needs are met according to God's riches in glory by Christ Jesus. (based on Philippians 4:19)

4. When I sow bountifully, I reap bountifully. (based on 2 Corinthians 9:6)

5. My seed yields thirty, sixty, and a hundredfold return for me. (based on Mark 4:8)

6. The Lord supplies seed for me to sow and bread for my food. He multiplies my seed for sowing and increases the fruit of my righteousness. (based on 2 Corinthians 9:10)

7. The Lord increases me a thousandfold more than I am, and blesses me just as He has promised. (based on Deuteronomy 1:11)

8. I have been given life in abundance and I will not lack. (based on John 10:10)

9. When I give out, it is given back to me – pressed down, shaken together, and running over. (based on Luke 6:38)

10. I remember the Lord my God, for it is He who gives me the power to make wealth, that He may confirm His covenant. (based on Deuteronomy 8:18)

11. The Lord empowers me by the power of the Holy Spirit to work provisional miracles in His name and to proclaim His testimonies with boldness. (based on Acts 1:8)

12. Like Jesus when He multiplied the loaves and the fish, the replenishment miracle unto increase operates freely and efficiently in my life every time I exercise my faith unto that end. (based on Mark 6:33-44; John 14:12)

RECORD OF REPLENISHMENT MIRACLES

Description of Seed (Date sown, money, time, service, quantity, etc.)	Description of Replenishment (Date replenished, quantity and circumstances.)

RECORD OF REPLENISHMENT MIRACLES

Description of Seed (Date sown, money, time, service, quantity, etc.)	Description of Replenishment (Date replenished, quantity and circumstances.)

RECORD OF REPLENISHMENT MIRACLES	
Description of Seed (Date sown, money, time, service, quantity, etc.)	Description of Replenishment (Date replenished, quantity and circumstances.)

RECORD OF REPLENISHMENT MIRACLES	
Description of Seed (Date sown, money, time, service, quantity, etc.)	Description of Replenishment (Date replenished, quantity and circumstances.)

RECORD OF REPLENISHMENT MIRACLES

Description of Seed (Date sown, money, time, service, quantity, etc.)	Description of Replenishment (Date replenished, quantity and circumstances.)

A Patricia King Institute Course

One of many great courses available

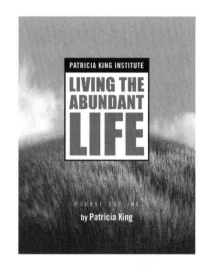

There seems to be some controversy and confusion around the term "prosperity" in the body of Christ, but there was none with Christ Himself. He made it clear. He came so we might have an abundance of life. And the apostle Paul wrote that we were to prosper and be in health. Isn't it time, beloved, that you left lack behind?

Join Patricia King for this course, *Living the Abundant Life*, and be mentored on how to step into supernatural provision to enjoy the blessing, prosperity and abundance of all Jesus has made available to you – love, joy, peace, favor, mercy, grace, provision, protection, health, strength, and every good thing!

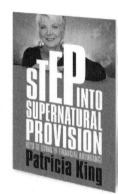
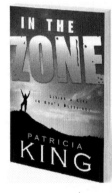

Decree the Word!

Decree a thing and it shall be established.

Job 22:28

The Word of God is powerful and it will profoundly influence your life. It accomplishes everything that it is sent to do.

Patricia King wrote *Decree* to help believers activate the power of the Word in key areas of their lives, including health, provision, love, victory, and wisdom, to name a few.

Unlock Your Life's Full Potential!

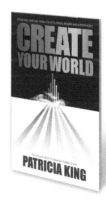

Create Your World will empower you to frame your world and experience the kind of life Jesus died to give you. Extraordinary truths are presented with clear and simple guidelines to live a life of victory rather than a life of defeat.

As you read and apply the principles, your relationships, health, finances, and overall state of being will be supernaturally blessed by God!

About Patricia King

Patricia King is a respected apostolic minister of the gospel and has been a pioneering voice in ministry, serving for over 30 years as a Christian minister in conference speaking, prophetic service, church leadership, and television and radio appearances. She is the founder of Patricia King Ministries, Women in Ministries Network and Patricia King Institute, the co-founder of XPmedia.com, and director of Women on the Frontlines. She has written many books, produced numerous CDs and DVDs, and hosts her TV program *Patricia King – Everlasting Love*. She is also a successful business owner and an inventive entrepreneur. Patricia's reputation in the Christian community is world-renowned.

To Connect:

Patricia King website: PatriciaKing.com

Facebook: Facebook.com/PatriciaKingPage

Patricia King Institute: PatriciaKingInstitute.com

Women on the Frontlines and Women in Ministry Network: Woflglobal.com

Patricia King – Everlasting Love TV Program and many other video teachings by Patricia: XPmedia.com

50813662R00038

Made in the USA
San Bernardino, CA
04 July 2017